REFLECTIVE SPECTRUM

Cherylanne Arnott

Copyright © 2018 by Cherylanne Arnott.

All rights reserved. No part of this publication may be reproduced, distributed, or transmitted in any form or by any means, including photocopying, recording, or other electronic or mechanical methods, without the prior written permission of the author, except in the case of brief quotations embodied in critical reviews and certain other noncommercial uses permitted by copyright law.

Printed in the United States of America

ISBN: 978-1-948172-73-8 (Paperback)
ISBN: 978-1-948172-72-1 (eBook)

Library of Congress Control Number: 2018945889

Stonewall Press
363 Paladium Court
Owings Mills, MD 21117
www.stonewallpress.com
1-888-334-0980

This book is dedicated to my incredible friend Sarah: with her unwavering support and feedback, she's been my best critic, council, and anchor.

Author's Comment

Someone once said, "To write well, you have to write what you know." This is what I know: The Good, The Bad, and The Ugly ... (a little something for everyone)

To reach out and touch you (with your own thoughts) in the *Reflective Spectrum*.

Contents

Acknowledgements ix
Introduction xi

Chapter One: The Good 1
Chapter Two: The Bad 53
Chapter Three: 'The Ugly' 75

Acknowledgements

I wish to recognize and thank my wonderful family and my incredible friends for their ongoing support, critiques and enthusiasm in this and all my endeavors.

I wish to thank my son Nicolas, my Aunt Marianne, and Uncle Vince, my cousin Dr. Vince, my friend Lalonna, my friends Dean and Paula, Sarah (my anchor), and Juliana.

And I wish to thank Stonewall Press for their patience, guidance, input, and creativity in bringing my dream to life.

Introduction

Kaleidoscopic:
The Coalescence...of Dreams
...in the Spectrum Suite.

Like Painted Echoes
in a Hidden Memory...
my Muse Awakens.

What can I say? My Muse has saved me Thousands of Hours...{and Dollars} in Psychotherapy... lol, but True!! So, Thank You my Muse: for this Therapeutic Outlet for Emotions...Let's only Hope Readers derive Insight, Inspiration, and the Comfort that they are not Alone...

CHAPTER ONE

The Good 'Happy Thoughts'

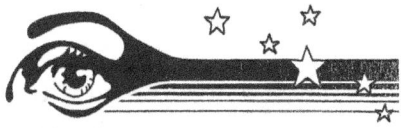

Cherylanne Arnott

...like Painted echoes
in a Hidden Memory;
my Muse...Awakens...

Tigers in the House
Roam with Softly Padded Feet
Secrets...in their Eyes

Mystical Crystals;
shining Rainbows in the rooms
Kaleidoscope Walls

Autumn Winds are here
Sun burnt Leaves swirl 'round and down
Carpeting the Ground

Miss Fall is Painting
the Splashed Countryside Reflects
Her own Abstract Dreams

I bury my Face...
in the Strength of His Shoulders
to plant Love's Soft Kiss

Thirteen Thousand Knots:
each contains a Fantasy;
Happiness...with You!

Slow, Rippling Water
lapping upon Pebbly Sand...
Rests my mind...in Peace

Crickets chirp mellow
against the Night's Soft Breezes:
Sing on...little ones

He...Looks at me with
Lusty Sparks in his Dark Eyes
Love Sprouts as Hearts Pound

Cherylanne Arnott

Got the Lover's Blues...
Missing Him: deep into Night:
{wish we were Pressed Close!}

How it Blows out there!!
the Storm rustles up dead leaves:
Bittersweet Memories...

Time passes quickly
for Lovers...in their Passion
...fully Spent...Content

Little Golden Rings
Encircle all my Fingers
Presents...from my Love

Clothed in Wakefullness
I Ride the Night...next to You...
a Place...to Belong

Sacred Night; New Fire...
Harmonious Convergence
...from my Book of Dreams

dancing with Shadows
in a Secret World...I Wait...
Thinking...about You

Addicted to You:
Complete Intoxication
this very Moment

a Promise of Love:
Whispers...in the afternoon:
Caressed by the Wind

something about You...
Let the Wheel of Fortune Spin...
Journey...to the Heart

Cherylanne Arnott

Quiet Reflections:
...the Other Side of Silence
in the Afterglow...

My Voice Rides the Wind:
...Invitation from Within:
...I need you: Tonight...

Visions and Voices
Wait for Me...on Trails of Dreams:
Future Memories

Never Surrender.
Begin Again. Begin Now.
...I'm growing my Wings

Anticipation:
and when at Last I Hold You;
Perfect Alignment

Fire...in the Rainstorm:
when I look into Your Eyes;
Sacred Alliance

the Search...is Over.
You were with me All the While
{Saved the Best for Last!}

in my Secret Heart
the Search has come full Circle:
All Roads Lead to You.

Angels...on the Wind...
a World...of Private Music;
...Language of the Soul

in Sunrise I walk...
...a Butterfly in the Well
Dazzled by the Light

We've got Tonight' Babe
...let me Hold you...in my Arms:
Heartsong Lullaby

this Moment: this Chance;
Filled...with Possibilities...
...a New Dawn Rising...

Virgin Timber Stands:
Ladies in Waiting to the
Bagby Hot Springs Bums

when I was Sleeping...
You were With Me...All the While
Bring on the Wonder!!

Take Life as it Comes
...Heaven IS a Place on Earth:
Garden of Delight

Feelings Ignited:
so Strong...so Simple...so Deep
...Colors...of the Heart

Forever your Girl
through some Miracle of Fate:
...Fantasy...made Real...

all I Want...is You!!
Envelope me...in your Soul:
Nothing Else...but Now

in Each Other's Arms...
Everything...is Good...and Safe...
and getting Better

You're Calling to Me:
with every Beat of my Heart
I Hear...the Magic

Rhythm...of the Night;
makin' Love...to each Other...
when the Feelin's Right

Please...Whisper to Me...
one Lover to Another:
No One...in between

Awaken...the Dawn
Morning Grace...Beauty and Fire
..a new Horizon

Quiet Certainty
I have Fallen: Deep...and Hard
{here I go Again!}

Come...take my Hand, now
...let this Spell last...Forever
what you See...is Real

Reflective Spectrum

Doorway to a Dream:
the End...of the Innocence
...take my Breath away...

in Quiet Moments
Imagination Whispers
Kaleidoscope Thoughts

Waterfall Cascade...
Holographic Tapestry
in Fluid Motion

...with Ancient Wisdom
I can See...your True Colors:
...that which Lies Within

like a Kiss of Fire
You...are my Sweet Emotion;
Fantasy made Real

the Wheels...are Turning
whatever will Be will Be
Relax...and Enjoy

Spangles of Sunshine
Explode into Existence
at the Break of Day

Corridors of Dreams...
a Rich Sea...of Sensation,
Texture, and Detail

Achingly Intense:
the Waiting...is...Delicious;
Exquisite Longings

Tenderly Maintained
in the Bedrock of the Heart:
Secret Fantasies

Reflective Spectrum

in Clean White Starfire
MoonShadows Dance like Fairies
Leaping...into Flight

a Moment of Grace
in the Music of Laughter
{Provides Sweet Relief}

Imagination:
...it's the Place...where dreams come True!
Listen. and Create

can't Fight this Feeling
Relentless. and Powerful
Invigorating

that Spark...of Mischief
when I Touched your Hand
Embers...became Fire!

Fragile. and Distant
a Moment...of Perfection
in Veils of Shadow

this Sweet Surrender...
making Love the Whole Night Through
fully Spent. Content.

within the Silence
a Door...between Dimensions
Ancient Memories

Detach...and Become:
stepping across the Threshold
into the Rainbow

Synchronicity...
for a tenuous Moment
all's Right with the World

Reflective Spectrum

Gathering Courage
Quivering with Excitement
Losing all the Tears

Smooth...and Sensuous
too Delicious to Resist:
Your Lips...Sweet Surprise!!

You...are like Lightening
with Sudden Thunder and Fire
...Melting into Me...

a Sudden Insight:
the Brink of Discovery
Glowing...with Pale Fire

Interstellar Space
so Achingly Beautiful
Strangely Enchanted

Bright with Reflections
the Night seems Filled with Magic
and Auras of Mystery

the Subconscious Mind
riding Currents of the Night
{Dreams are the Doorways}

a Brief, Sweet Madness
a little bit of Nonsense
what more could one ask??

Erotic Promise:
Sudden Thunder in the Heart
...Clothed in Shrouds of Fire

the Message...is Clear.
Lose Ourselves...in Wild Romance
Live the Fantasy

from Mists in my Mind
...a Looming Revelation!!
Instant. and Profound

Reflective Spectrum

Golden Glimmerings
ignite the Fuses of Hope
with Childlike Wonder

Live Another Life
...an Appealing Enterprise
...a different Light

a New Corridor
as Thin as a Razor Slash
filled...with Reckless Hope

like a Great Treasure
Indomitable Spirit
{a Psychic Totem}

Surprising Triumphs
simple Shifts of Perspective
the Crucial Detail

Tempered by the Fire
now...All Things are Possible
Divine Alignment

Seek Serenity
the Heart's Illumination
a Celebration

the Kiss...of Sunlight
Luminous Awakening
Healing...for the Soul

every Rose has Thorns
...back from Ruin...to Glory
Fate evens things out

a Crazy Yearning
for the Thrill...of Adventure
...Utterly...Reckless

I have Transcended
the Peak of Hysteria
Trembling...with Relief

Desire...to Survive
that's the Essence of the Game
the Source...of Power

like a Jeweled Belt
a Lingering Memory
...Lavishly Detailed

Rebuilding the Dream
through Logic and Reflection
...with the Spice of Tears

Subliminal Clues
now Revealing greater Depths
Brighter and Clearer

Return to Balance
by Virtue of Common Sense
Zen Simplicity!!

Constant and Intense:
Temptations to Embrace Hope
Soar to the Surface

the Hourglass of Time
...where Secret Dramas Unfold...
Minute... by... Minute

Vividly Recalled:
fragments... of a Deeper Dream
...Genuine Revelations

Sudden and Complete:
return to Stability:
...Astonished Delight!!

Tremendous Power
Shimmering... like a Mirage
through a Silver Rain

a Wistful Desire...
Considerable Pleasure...
a Touch... of Magic

Motivating Force:
a Ray... of Enlightenment:
the Courage... to Jump

to have the Last Laugh
in Spite of Desperation:
...Absolute Freedom

Cherylanne Arnott

Release the Hinges:
the Other Side of the Door
has Spectrums of Light

in Spite of the Dread...
the Passion... is in the Risk:
...Possibilities...

Stardust Tapestry
Painting the Vault of the Night
Bright with Mystery

at the Edges of Vision
an Intriguing Dimension
Darkly Glistening

Never-Ending Search
to find the Proper Prism:
the Meaning of Life

Reflective Spectrum

Scintillant Display
in Remarkable Detail:
Colorful Twilight

an Eerie Beauty...
Mysterious...and Haunting...
White Wings of Stormlight

Whispers... in the Wind:
Secrets... from another Realm;
Inspiration's Born

Secret Rendezvous!!
Anticipation's Tingle
Achingly Tender

Transcendental Truths
Brilliant... and Visionary
will Balance the Scales

Walking in the Light
with Wild Exhilaration:
a State... of Rapture

Imagination:
a Coat of many Colors
each Thread... Essential

Never Surrender.
this Moment's Ferocity
...Invulnerable...

Honesty to Self:
a Sacred Obligation
...to the Final Phase

the Nighttime's Release:
slip over the Edge...of Sleep:
Ultimate Mercy

Reflective Spectrum

Altered Perceptions
Mesmerizing... and Daring:
Strangely Seductive

find your Destiny:
some will Win... and some will Lose:
Never Stop Searching

Bright Reality:
the Potential for Success
it is Always... Now

Shifting Filigree
Higher Realms of Consciousness
are Always Churning

just Dusting off Dreams
and... Living on a Prayer;
with Urgent Purpose

sudden Rush... of Hope:
renewed Purity of Soul...
almost... Jubilant

the Darkness Brightens:
Personal Revelations
fill the Emptiness

on the Wings of Love
is the Only Way to Fly
Silent Certainty

a Time... for Healing...
on the Grace of Eagle's Wings
...Metamorphosis

Passion's Purity:
let's Perfect our Chemistry
Somewhere... in the Night

Reflective Spectrum

come to your Senses!!
Regain Equilibrium
...Conscious Intention...

Sketches... of the Dream:
little pieces of my Soul
from another Time

don't stop Believing;
there's a Bright Pearl to be Found
in the Dragon's Lair

that Moment in Time...
Waiting... for a Star to Fall
in Sparks and Embers

a Fleeting Moment
from behind the Wall of Doubt
...Fragile Happiness

as tho a Mirage:
Subliminal Perceptions...
Implicit Meanings

God's Always with me
Loved Him a thousand Lifetimes:
I'm Never Alone

in Refuge of Sleep...
the Gate to Eternity
is Hidden... in Dreams

Magnificent Light:
Ethereally Beautiful...
the Rainbow's Mural

Compelled to Follow
a Wordless, Silent Summons
into the Temple

Surrender Control:
let's Fall... the Rest of the Way:
Perfect Alignment

the Awakening:
Live the Life you've Imagined
Everything...is Now

Once upon a Time
Endless Possibilities:
Miraculous Chance!!

the Day of Release:
this Miraculous Passage
...like an Avalanche

a Quiver of Light:
better to Hope...than to Despair
...Lever-Point Moments

Picturesque Music:
the Birds...Singing in the Dawn;
...a Celestial Touch

a River of Stars...
the Fabric of Destiny
in a Distant Place

One Round Pearl: the Moon
...pure Ambrosia for the Soul:
Bask...within its Light

Call of the Mountains:
Ascension...to Sacred Space:
Glimpse...of the Divine

a Steady Pulsing...
this Vision...Beyond the Light
...it's my Secret Muse

Reflective Spectrum

on Secret Missions
Birds...Winging over Wetlands
...Feathers Float to Earth...

Healing Broken Wings
Radiant Awakening:
Learning...to take Flight

Potential Allies;
Transcendence in Unity
...our Kindred Spirits

in these Lucid Dreams
distant Roads are Calling me
from the Otherworld

Bringers of the Dawn...
many Voices...One Spirit:
Nature's Music Box

Voices from Heaven
Angelic Circle Chorale
Lullaby...from Home

Myself...on a bench
sharing Spring Morning with a
Robin on the rock

Windblown Waves of Grass...
Flowering Trees bend and sway:
Blankets of Petals

Drifting...inside Dreams
Angelic Wings Surround me
in the State of Grace

Silvery Laughter:
Wind-chimes hung out by Fairies
Dancing...in the Light

Reflective Spectrum

Angelic Embrace:
Sweet, dissolving Edge of Bliss;
Grace Personified

Instrumental Dreams...
Altered States of Consciousness:
just Waking the Muse...

Testing these new Wings
this Dream's Manifestation:
Return to Freedom

Whirlybirds spiral
looking like a Dragonfly
...Imagination

the day is Gloaming
Birds are Singing Lullabies...
Nestlings Dream...of Flight

Cherylanne Arnott

Diaphanous Clouds
Tendrilling around the Moon
playing Peek-a-Boo

Dawn's far from Quiet
a Cacaphony of Sound
Bird Song Fingerprints

My own back dooryard
a Slice...of this Whole Planet
is contained Within

in Dappled Sunlight
amongst Flora and Fauna
Fairies are Flitting

Quiet Reflections
Secret Gardens offer Peace:
a Time for Healing

Reflective Spectrum

Valley...in the Clouds
powdered with Silvery Light
Dawn Imaginings

Caring. Commitment.
the Purpose of Existence:
Choices...that we Make

Moonlight on Water
an Alluring Oasis
Cool...and Smooth as Silk

Glimpses of Heaven
Vivid, Solid, and Profound:
Explosion...of Faith

Unspoken Subtext:
Startling Realizations
{such Similar Souls!!}

the Loom...of the Night:
Descending Oblivion...
...Protective Nimbus...

Skies before the Storm:
the Artist's Inner Struggle
Torrential Release

out of Wind and Fire
in another Place and Time
the Goddess...Rising

Enough...is Enough:
in one Swift, Graceful Movement
an End...to Secrets

Break the Chains of Fear
offer up your Best Defense
with Enchanted Swords

Cloud Imaginings
prepare to be Enchanted
with Childlike Wonder

a Smile...from your Lips...
just Lovers...in the Moonlight:
I Thirst no more

Let's Capture the Dream
and bring the Legend to Life:
...Untie the Ribbon!!

Wordless Urgency:
a Pure, Intense Emotion
Deeper than Desire

Wings over Water
Firefly Fairy Lanterns Flash
...Luminaria...

Heart of the Castle:
Repository of Dreams
within the Portals

Out of the Ashes
Surprising Revelations
Soul's Awakening

Transcendent Spirit
Tremendous Liberation
Totally Transformed

Come into the Light...
undergo a Tidal Change
Blossoming Breakthrough

Visions...and Healing:
a Special Intensity:
Cosmic Energy

Reflective Spectrum

a New Kind of Love:
Trembling Edge of Happiness
...just Feel the Journey

the Patterns of Fate
are Inextricably Linked
Listen...with your Heart

Afternoon Delight:
Magical Discoveries
...out of Fairy Tales

Invisible Touch
...it's Ambient Alchemy:
what Dreams are made of

Manicured Talons
leave Red Welts on Tender Skin
{small Price for such Lust!}

Cherylanne Arnott

Billowing White Sea
stretches Endless, 'neath the Ship
an Ocean...of Clouds

Glass -Ribbon Highway
winds 'round Thoughts of my True Love
and into the Night

Wisps of Lace-White Snow
traces Corners of the Rooftops
Ghosts...of last night's Storm

Lips softly Gleaming
in the Candlelight tonight:
Tickle...my...Fancy

the Silver Blimp Sails
through Charcoal-Purple Clouds like
a Whale...in the Sea

Reflective Spectrum

Chips clicking softly
while the Players Deal the Cards
Smoky room...hushed Bets

Sun-White is the Moon
as She Dances in the Hills
Chasing the Shadows

Red Satin Pillows
help me Dream of You with Lust
...and Long for your Touch

your Wonderful Eyes
look into my Soul; leave me
Moaning. Soft...and Low

Living Cat-Statue
sits in the Shade of the Pine
blinking Jade-Green Eyes

Blankets piled High, but
it's not Warm to sleep Alone:
Hungry...for your Touch

Dragons in the Clouds
stir up the Morning Thunder:
the Bear...seeks his Cave

the High Priestess Laughs
as her Belly Undulates
{it Tickles inside}

my Thoughts Rest on you
Lascivious Abandon!!
Fantasies Fulfilled

Orphaned by the Storm:
you've brought me Back to Life...from
a Land beyond Tears

Reflective Spectrum

Sparkles in your eyes
mean that you're in Love with Me
Bound. Eternally.

I'm over my head
into this Love-Lust with you
but...it sure feels...nice

You...have the Power
to make me Cry...with Desire
{if you only Knew!!}

You...are my True Love
I've waited Years to find you:
Never go Away!!

Savor the Moment
Live the Fantasy...with Me!!
for all that it's Worth!!

Ah!! my Sweet Lover!!
you Inspire within my Soul
the Pain of Desire!!

be a Part of Me
to have you here beside me
makes me Shine Inside

your Voice on the phone
Touching me...across the Miles
helps me through Long Nights

Come...and Fly with Me:
I'll give to you...All Pleasures
on the Wings of Love

Long Live the Showgirls!!
they bring Glamour back to Life
and set Hearts on Fire!!

being 'Whore at Heart"
I Love All of my Lovers
Each One...for Theirself

seems Light Years away
until I can Be with you:
...I count the minutes!!

my Sometimes Lover
Oh! why must you Tease me, thus!!
it's so Hard to Wait

when I'm Without you
I hold you Close...in my Dreams
Singing you Love Songs

when you're Holding me
you Light a Fire in my Soul
that Burns once you've Gone

Cherylanne Arnott

Burning...with Desire
I Wait for you...in the Night
{can you Feel my Love??}

Anticipation
as I wait to Hear your Voice
minutes...seem like Hours

Forgive me, my Love
for All my Indiscretions
{my Heart's yours Alone}

this Thought I leave you
the Legacy of our Love
Spans the Universe

the She-Spider spins
the most Delicate Daydreams
at the Web's Center

Blue Jays come to munch
the seeds I've strewn upon Rocks
their Pleasure...and Mine!!

seems like Yesterday
I left my Heart...in your Bed
so Many Years Gone

Fantasy Lover
Weaves my Dreams into the Dawn
Harvesting the Winds

Flashdancer Struts it
through the Raunchy Honky-Tonks
bathed in Fire and Ice

Strum into the Night
the Golden Hair of my Lute
...Wizard of Octaves...

my Thoughts Rest on you
many Times during the Day
you've Captured my Heart!!

Leaves are Floating down
Crowning my head with Colors
Autumn Dreams Abound

Shadows...out of Time
like the Tongues of Wild Children
Muffled...by the Reeds

Watercolor Moon
tonight's the Time for Secrets
Miracles made Real

Thunder and Roses
a Knight in Shining Armor
the Lady...in Red

Reflective Spectrum

the Alteration:
a Coat of many Colors
Illustrated Men

Streaking Black and Rust
across the Open Meadow
Black Brandy Flashes

the Shape of Desire
Creature of Light...and Darkness
Daughter of the Earth

the Umbra's Rising
Cold Moon over Atlantis
Valley of Shadows

from Deepest Fathoms
Effortless, Liquid Movements
the Mermaid's Children

Pastel Lady in
the Gaze of the Unicorn
Tapestry of Love

Candle...in the Wind
Woman...on the Hem of Time:
all Freedom and Grace

Early Morning Snow
Diamonds falling from the Sky
Glimmerings of Grace

Puerto Rican Prince
Bittersweet, Chocolate Skin
Poem Speaking Mouth

Priceless Possession:
the Fire of Youth...at its Dawn
so Unquenchable

Reflective Spectrum

a Dream that Once was
Woven on the Loom of Fate:
the Stuff of Legends

an Innocent Heart:
the Lamp which Lightens the Soul
with Love's Clairvoyance

Chinese Lullaby
Fascinating Fairy Realm...
Enchanting Puppets

Silky Nebula
wrapped up in Silent Wonder
there will come Soft Rains...

Lightening Lights the Skies
with Fire hanging from the Clouds
a Fearsome Tempest

Cherylanne Arnott

Pot-Bellied Cupids
Capering with the Satyrs
Frolic Fits of Mirth

Palpitating Hopes:
the Wonder of Innocence
against All the Odds

Wine...in a Goblet:
Twilight...in Grey Velvet Shoes:
farr-off Reflections

a Leap beyond Time:
the Majesty of Virtue
Wiping the Slate Clean

CHAPTER TWO

The Bad
{Cognitive Dissonance}

Cherylanne Arnott

the Days...are the Same
they Come...and Go. Without Hope
I'm Screaming Inside

I am So Afraid
let me Rest...a little While
and I'll Face the World

I Cry...in Despair
for our Lost and Broken Hearts
Silently Bleeding

Unrequited Love
Taunts Open all the old Scars
Anew. Searing Hot.

the Skull's Empty Eyes
Stare at me...across the Room
Echoing my Thoughts

Reflective Spectrum

I get so Restless
in my Lonesome Glass Prison
and long for a Friend

Impossible Dreams
Overwhelming Sadness for
the Lonely Lady

the Show Must go on:
...but it's all an Illusion
as she Weeps inside

Life's Game...is Constant:
no Allowances for Lovers
...when the Chips re Down

all this Wasted Time!!
...days are Nothing without you...
Longing for your Touch

Insanity Laughs...
...the Edge of a Broken Heart
Longing for Shelter

I Fell...through the Cracks
Headfirst...into...Emptiness
of Windows in Time

there's so Many Ways
every Memory Repeats
Rolling, like Thunder

...like a Broken Child...
Layers and Layers of Pain
are Wet...with my Tears

Always Remember
...in Dense Tears and Heavy Sobs
Loves...that I have Lost

...Uncontrollable...
Raging Fury...Deep Inside:
...when the Laughter Stops

...Profound Sense of Loss
Pieces...of a Shattered Life:
Never be the Same

my Fury's Rising:
Thunder...is Shaking these Bones
Again...and Again

the Sun...at Midnight
my Eyes...that see in the Dark
Cry...like a Rainstorm

Every Little Step
...Hard...and Scary...and Brutal
beyond this Moment

...an Eternal Void:
owner of a Broken Heart
Walking...between Worlds

there's a Storm Raging
through my Broken Heart tonight
...Point of No Return

a Sweet Wistfulness
echoes in my Memory
just Beneath the Surface

Childhood Fantasies
...Unpolluted. Crystalline.
Vanishing...in Mists

Quiet Emptiness
Listening...to the Silence
astride the Two Worlds

Reflective Spectrum

a Rite of Passage:
the Door to Understanding
through Hard-Won Insights

a Soul...in Torment:
I stand between two Doorways:
a Private Elsewhere

Wandering the Night
Enveloped in Memories
the Clock...has no Hands

Echoes...across Time
like Whisperings in the Walls
Scuttle through the Mind

like a Fading Star
from a Dream Within a Dream
Memories...of Love

Effectively Trapped
in a Random Fold in Time
Hostage...to Fortune

like Forlorn Spirits...
just Me...and my Shadow-Self
Restlessly Pacing

as Brittle as Ice:
an Element...of Chaos
Perilously Close

Exhausted Courage:
...in a Storm of Emotions
Logic...is Slipping

like a Raven's Wing
Murkey...in Spite of Sunshine:
a Soul...in Shadows

Reflective Spectrum

a Hidden Chamber
found on the Dark Side of Sleep:
the Innermost Self

Lightening Scars the Sky
Around. and Down...and Away...
a Bright Reflection

a Daliesque World...
this Storm...between Birth...and Death:
...Quicksilver Puddles...

a Wallowing Mood:
Profoundly Disquieting;
this Downward Spiral

like Murmured Chanting
in the Sound of Breaking Surf
Strangled sounds of Grief

Cherylanne Arnott

Harboring Dark Truths
sometimes the Laughter will Hurt
...such Blithe Treachery

Faceless Pursuer:
just a Phantom...in a Dream
a Dark Enchantment

Demented Impulse:
...stepping through the Looking-Glass
back...into the Storm

the Cold Void...of Truth:
maybe Choice...is an Illusion:
a Desperate Hope

Mask...of Sanity
Emotional Pollution
Piercing the Facade

Reflective Spectrum

the Tide...is Turning
toward my own Strange Destiny
in Churning Currents

Pure Love...and Patience:
...the Last, Precious Emotions
Faded...to Whispers

Destiny Revealed
with a Shattering Coldness
it's Cosmic Justice

Wonder...and Courage
reverberate through the Mind
...but there Are Nightmares

Fear...tempered by Hope
with a Sadness at the Core
...a Fatal Error

Cherylanne Arnott

Leave this Waking Dream
Safety is an Illusion
Adjust to the Loss

like Discarded Toys
the Songs of the Inner Child
...a Pile of Rubble

this Transient Madness!!
it's a Trick...of Perspective
all Cracked and Canted

Fearless; but Haunted;
Prepare...for Confrontation
with no Illusions

the Mind...is Quicksand
Feverish with Frustration
Unpredictable

Reflective Spectrum

Snared in a Nightmare
I Dreamt the Impossible:
Dervish Shadows Whirl

Outside...looking in
Windows...to a Haunted Place:
a Precinct...of Hell

the Bliss...of Being
Somewhere back there...in the Dust
...Disintegrating...

Songs...of Enchantment??
Nothing...but a Deception:
a little Charade

with Mute Endurance
like the Bones of Slain Dragons
Echoes...from the Past

Cherylanne Arnott

Eclipse...of the Heart:
let me take a Long...Last Look
...Unspeakably Sad

Deep. and Deceptive:
...it's a Long Road...to Heaven:
Formidable Odds

Enchanted Whispers
both Dazzling...and Darkling:
Conflicting Desires

back on the Treadmill:
the Days...mount to Centuries:
Relentless Patterns

Ferocious Currents
...know the Fury...of the Storm
...Dire Confrontations

Reflective Spectrum

Dark…and Bittersweet
{just like an old Love Affair}
…this Confused Despair

I'll Swallow my Tears
Patterns of Reflection are
Slippery when Wet

Fiercely Insistent
Ghost Mail…from the Other Side
Ceaseless and Vivid

Tides of Emotion:
Cheap Sentimentality
…only Graffiti

a Tender Spirit
so Small…so Vulnerable
Battered by the Wind

Cherylanne Arnott

these Nighttime Journeys
not merely Innocent Fun
...a Profound Level

Falling...and Feeling
I'm waiting...to Catch the Light
Constant Illusion

Phantom Carousel
Spider Webs, Silence, and Dust
no Solidity

Edge of Eternal...
my Soul's Whispering to me:
...we've got Each Other

in Secret Spaces
Silence...between my two Worlds
...the Vanishing Point

Reflective Spectrum

on a Strange Highway
13 Seconds...to Nowhere
in this Twilight Zone

Rest First. Think Later.
Pain...turns into Memory
Mists...within a Mist

Savage Therapy
Anger: the Engine of Change
Hope...for a New Life

Metamorphosis:
Ultimate Revelations
...are often Fatal

a Strange, Whispered Phrase
Vibrates in the Memory
Insinuation

Cherylanne Arnott

a Fiendish Temper:
eyes of Infernal Luster
the Black Magician

the Grumbling Tide
Elusive...but Insistent
Fearsome in its Wrath

Silent as Fox-Fire
something Wicked this way comes
the Small Assassin

Sarcasm's Saber:
the Cutting Edge...of the Mind
which Cleaves Hearts in Two

Swaddled in Darkness
these Exquisite Fantasies
dispel their Magic

Reflective Spectrum

as Wildfire with Wind
in the Eye of the Cyclone
a Soul in Torment

Lost Inspiration
bowed under the Weight of Time:
a Throbbing Echo

Devil's Advocate
Programmed for Pathology
with Forbidden Thoughts

Tunnel in the Sky:
a Mirror for Observers
the Rape of the Moon

the Devil's Cheval:
Journey into Illusion
Distempered Fantasies

Cherylanne Arnott

Eyes do more than See:
you can Run...but you can't Hide:
a Case of Conscience

all Stumbles and Hugs
old Friends of the Family
Nothing in Common

Dancer in the Flames
the Phoenix...and the Mirror
a Shattered Goddess

Spiraling Downwards
in a Patternless Tattoo
Insanity Laughs

in Bits and Pieces
I have Endured the Labyrinth
Alone...with the Fire

Beware Alcohol
Embrace this Liquid Lover
there is No Escape

in Starlight and Frost
previous Reflections hold
Smiles. of Coldest White

I can Hear the Dark
Distinctly Disquieting:
a Heart...between Beats

CHAPTER THREE

'The Ugly'
{Descent into Madness}

{Reader Discretion Advised}

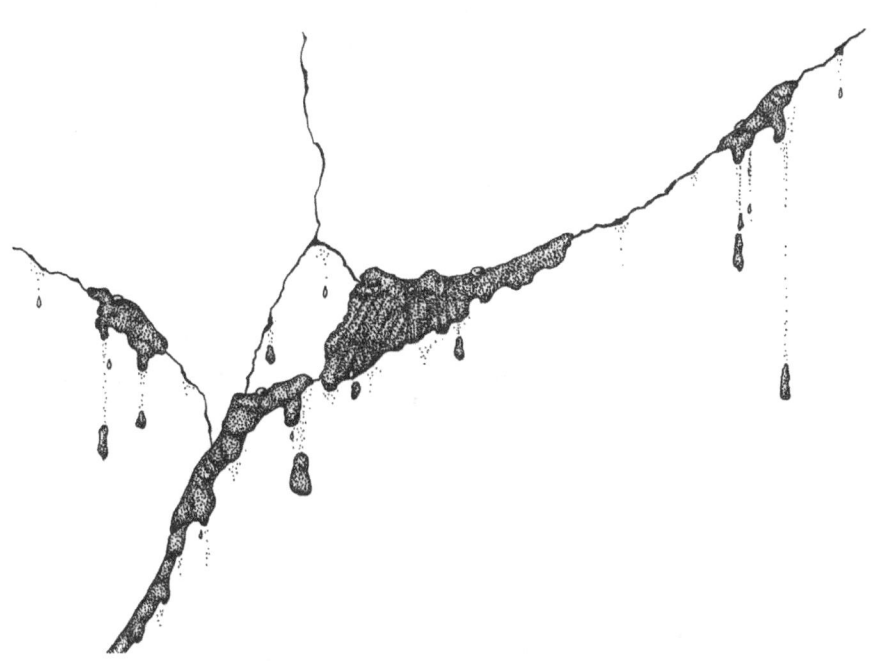

Riding the Nightmare...
Someday...I'll Wake up Dead
the Descent...Complete

Dark...and Merciless...
Moonless Midnight of the Mind:
a Howling Bedlam

Sharp...as a Razor
Deeper than Eternity:
Anger. and Sadness

Rude Awakening
into Cold Reality:
Shaking...and Frantic

Spectral Energy:
the Beating Heart...of Nightmares:
Shadows, Ghosts, and Smoke

Words Cut...like a Sword
Potent as Cobra Venom:
Deadly. and Intense

Lost...in Emotions
Bordering on Lunacy
Surrender...to Tears

in the Hostile Night;
Pain...and Fear...Muddle Reason:
Floodgates...to...Madness

Weak and Depleted:
Hugging Myself: and Rocking:
Sobbing...with no Sound...

Soul-shriveling Screams
in Final Desperation
...the Realm...of Ashes

Tumult and Turmoil:
Inexpressibly Intense:
this Ceaseless Struggle

...it's just Not Worth it...
...wanna Pull that Trigger. Now.
...to Oblivion

this State of Distress
a Black Hole...within Myself:
Bleakness...at the Core

Barbed Wire Scars my Heart
with Grief too Intense for Tears
...as if Sheathed in Ice

Increased Recklessness
in Extreme Circumstances:
Constant Jeopardy

Reflective Spectrum

Blades of Memory
Drifting up from the Deep Place
with Merciless Force

with Blood...and Thunder:
Anger is...Greater...than Fear
Sometimes...it's Justice

Dry-Rot...of the Soul...
the Deep...and Quiet Sadness
like a Tinderbox

a Gross Injustice
the Residue...Stains my Mind:
Extreme Overload

Blind Hostility
at the Backend of Nowhere:
Enormous Contempt

Cherylanne Arnott

the Death...of the Soul:
...Vortexes of Red-White Fire
in the Court of Hell

Compelled to Follow
Journeys down Endless Tunnels
Clotted...with Shadows

Curled around the Pain
of Desire...and Denial:
a Tremor...of Rage

with a Banshee Shriek
between Planes of Existence:
Unresolved Sorrow

Cruel...and Twisted:
...the Face...of Adversity
stirs Primitive Fears

Reflective Spectrum

Splinters...in my Heart:
Emotional Implosion
no Room left...for Tears

Agents of Chaos:
Emotions...Cloud your Feelings:
Fracturing the Mind

Wounded Warrior...
my Spirit Floats...in my Tears...
the Soul...remains Bruised

like Chilled Mercury:
Determined. Ruthless. Clever.
...that Cold...Savage...Self.

Hard Raps of Insight:
Deadly...as...a Stiletto:
Brutally Humbling

my Soul...is Broken...
a Descent into Darkness
filled...with Deep Silence

on the Verge of Tears...
Ensnared...by Tangled Visions:
Numb...with Exhaustion

Infinite Layers:
as Deep...as the Face of God:
Lingering Despair

Mercurial Moods:
Degrees...of Desperation
all the Way...to Hell

Blood. Death...and Rapture:
the Liberal Rules of Dreams:
...most Formidable

Reflective Spectrum

Wordless Wails...of Pain
Penitence...has been Suffered:
Genuine Anguish

a Hateful Wrongness:
a Furious Righteousness:
Virtuous Restraint

Vanquish your Rivals
the End...of the Innocence:
Victims...of the Game

Unrequited Love:
Eternity Suspended:
Exasperation

Fractured History:
Naught can fill the Hollowed Soul
Lost Decades Ago

Cold...as Frozen Steel:
a Chill...Rumbling through my Bones
as Brittle as Ice

Piercing Conclusion:
Reality's True Nature??
...another Wild Card

a Breaking...Inside
Empty Spaces...in the Heart
...seems Terribly Sad...

Enduring Anguish
Worn by the Teeth of Sorrow
Dark...with Unspent Rage

Mirror...of Madness:
Passed through my own Reflection
into Lunacy

Reflective Spectrum

as Black as Deep Space:
Sorrow...too Intense for Tears
a Cry...in the Night

a Remembered Cry:
Tears Move One as Fury can't:
Psychic Guillotine

Beyond Endurance:
an Emotional High-Wire
with Fatal Stress Cracks

Stark Confrontation:
Heart-Wrenching Revelations:
Merciless Moments

I'm Already Dead:
...and You're the One who Killed me:
my Wrath...will Haunt you

my World...is Silent
no more Laughter. no more Tears.
just this...Nothingness

we're not Done...just Yet:
Rage...doth Smolder...Forever
{better Watch your Back}

I See Forever:
...Screaming...into Emptiness:
Talkin'...to Myself

Twilight Solitude:
...now I'm Screamin'...in the Night
...Dreaming...in Real Time...

Mistress Alcohol
Lures, and then Robs, Rapes, and Wastes
in Her Dance of Death

Reflective Spectrum

as True as Despair
Order slips into Chaos
Welcome...to Abyss

my Heart's Neighborhood
on the Edge of Bitter Screams:
there's Blood on the Moon

Lambs...to the Slaughter:
this World's Wars...are made of Death:
Hollow Victories

all the Sounds of Fear:
Nothing's Something...Inside Out
Image...of the Beast

Eternally Sealed
in the Arms of Morpheus:
Frail Mortality

Cherylanne Arnott

an Eclipse of Mind
as through a Shattered Prism:
Deadly, Secret Fears

Forward and Perverse
Cunning deceives Ignorance
Banishing Reason

Vexation and Rage
Seduced by Civility:
Lament of Hatred

Wretched Existence!!
this Pathetic Fallacy
a Waking Nightmare

Tonight I find that
the Glass Shards of my Heart are
Leaking through my Eyes

www.ingramcontent.com/pod-product-compliance
Lightning Source LLC
Chambersburg PA
CBHW071532080526
44588CB00011B/1652